# THE VIG OF LOVE

BILL YARROW

To Emily,

What a pleasure to meet you
and hear you read!

Good luck with
the novel!

GLASS LYRE PRESS

All the best,

— Bill Yarrow

(10.18.18)

Vig: interest on a loan you will never repay

for Leah

Cover art:  Muradin | Dreamstime.com
Interior art: Volodymyr Tverdokhlib | Dreamstime.com
Author Photo: Leah Yarrow
Design & layout: Steven Asmussen
Copyediting: Linda E. Kim

Glass Lyre Press, LLC
P.O.  Box 2693
Glenview, IL 60026
www.GlassLyrePress.com

# CONTENTS

## Part One: Principal

A Debt No Honest Man Can Pay ............................ 15

Tierra Del Fuego ............................ 16

Auto Imperative ............................ 17

Ajloun Castle ............................ 18

The Exit Towards Fire ............................ 19

Crete ............................ 20

Andalusia ............................ 21

Augustinian Prayer Sonnet ............................ 27

Rattlesnake Pancakes ............................ 28

Mother and Son ............................ 30

We Don't Need No Education ............................ 31

When We Marry ............................ 32

Asbestos Candlestick ............................ 33

The Sober Boat ............................ 35

Poe/Pound Villanelle ............................ 36

The Basement of Desire ............................ 37

A Shadow on the Summer Sun ............................ 39

Walking Coma ............................ 41

The Man Whose Wife Lived In His Neck ............................ 42

# Part Two: Interest

| | |
|---|---|
| Five'll Get You Ten | 47 |
| Two Weeks in a Dristan Land | 48 |
| Everything the Traffic Will Allow | 49 |
| No Hay Bandaid | 52 |
| Epithalamion | 53 |
| Blackish by Reason of the Ice | 54 |
| Libby, Lottie, and Carlotta | 56 |
| Just the Facts | 57 |
| The Autobiography of the Falsehoods Which Are Not Love | 58 |
| Eleutheria | 59 |
| Maurice Utrillo | 60 |
| Absence | 61 |
| Sticky, Indifferent | 62 |
| Metro Retrofitting | 66 |
| The Beautiful Mercedes | 67 |
| The Ogontz Branch | 68 |
| Anniversary Waltz | 70 |
| Chattanooga Afternoon | 71 |
| 1st and Goal | 72 |

# Part Three: Accounts Payable

The Vig of Love                                77
Rising to the Bait                             78
Refrain from Embracing                         80
O, Brave New World!                            81
I'm Torn                                       83
Carlos!                                        85
Giving Up the Ghost                            87
It Can't Be, It Just Can't Be                  89
Spontaneous Tranquility                        90
Cranshaw at the Dinner Party                   91
Cranshaw Engages in Debate                     92
Cranshaw on a Boat                             93
Cranshaw on the Road                           94
Whorehouse, Anyone?                            95
The Best Banana Bread                          96
Addictions                                     97
Fealty                                        100
Call to Arms                                  101
Something He Wrote                            103
The Survival of the Bees                      104
The Concord of This Discord                   105
Noir vs. Noir                                 106

# Part Four: Accounts Receivable

| | |
|---|---|
| Wanna Bet? | 110 |
| Poem for Danny | 112 |
| The Assassination of Sadat | 114 |
| The Hardon Collider | 116 |
| The Rising Tide | 118 |
| Lunch Poem | 119 |
| Camp Atheism | 120 |
| The Knitting Needle | 121 |
| In the Seagull Colony | 122 |
| Beetle Tales | 123 |
| One Sick, Two Sick, Red Sick, Blue Sick | 126 |
| Bereft of Death | 128 |
| Laundry List | 129 |
| After Insouciance | 130 |
| Babble | 132 |
| Trompe L'Oeil | 133 |
| The Knife of Love is Never Blunt | 134 |
| The Secret of Belief | 136 |
| Pascal | 138 |

"Poetry is an axe"
—a student of Aristotle

# Part One: Principal

# A Debt No Honest Man Can Pay

I'm sitting here listening to *Nebraska* and it's
breaking my heart not because it's plaintive
and brilliant but because it's taking me back
to 1982 and our baby—not even two pounds—
in intensive care—in New York Hospital—far away
—we live in Queens—it's what we can afford—
but we see her every day—well one of us does—
via the subway—where I sit listening to *Nebraska*
and Springsteen is singing about paying a debt
no honest man can pay—and I'm thinking
*What is that debt? It's marriage, right? It's
love, right? It's the privilege of having a kid,
right? Not in the song but in life, in someone's
life, in my life, it is a debt, a brutally honest debt,
but you never pay it back, no one can, not with
money, not with time, not with compassion, not
with care, not with what I make, not even with
what you make, I'm not talking hospital bills,
I'm talking what forever can never be repaid*
so, listen, you listen to a song whose line hits you
in your kidney and you double over as if you're
pregnant—a pregnant woman—not close—not close
enough to term—but you birth something anyway
—and one day it becomes your heart—and then
your heart gets pregnant and it gives birth to
your future which you learn is made entirely
of your past, a past where you are listening to
a song, a concept, a whole album, again and
again, over and over, the album *Nebraska*, which
never gets dull, never gets tired, never gets old.

# TIERRA DEL FUEGO

what I remember most was how dark it was
at two in the morning and how angry the air
was at two in the morning and the sound
of sobbing in the trees at two in the morning

my time there was not one evening not one
river not one tunnel not one falling
it was not one body it was not one climate
not one lookout it was not one of anything

my residence was a rain of observation
a slim shower of speculation a felt resistance
in the soil a keen distance from the world
whose least reflex was a spongy corruption

when I landed I was frightened but not
unhappy I was apprehensive but not
unwilling the land left me with a shadow
of a longing left me hanging by acuity

then denial spoke and refusal erupted
the volatile earth got angry at depression's
lack of shame and sore abandon became
an argument I didn't have the energy to win

# Auto Imperative

I drove to you in April
and you loved me all through Illinois

I drove to you in April and even when the fender
was destroyed you loved me all through Illinois

I drove to you in April even when we lost
the radio you loved me all through Illinois

without the radio we drove we drove in each
other's voice and you loved me all through Illinois

without a radio without a fender
in the car I drove to you in April

with you beside me all through Illinois

# AJLOUN CASTLE

you my little cat are brisk and fluid
but I like an owl am stiff and staid
you clambered up the rocks and held out your arms
the wind in a swoosh came up behind you
incredulous I watched you fall

you did not see me looking
as you stood placid impassive
looking out over the cardamom hills
but then the wind mistook your arms
for wings and helpless I watched you fall

horrified I watched you fall
through the future and into the past
past your family past your accolades
past your handsome penchant for reconciliation
into the universal solvent of your confidence

I saw you dashed upon low stones!
I saw you bounce into the sea!
I saw you sink into inky velvet!

my tragedy is that my imagination
pictures all the facets of disaster

but you see only soaring
and that is your invincible gift

# THE EXIT TOWARDS FIRE

the world is black: I ignite
my eyes and arouse the false
darkness to jealousy

alone at the flash point
our longings expunge
the artificial light

ostracized time grows small
and cold as the ambition
of a flame

dark smoke billows from
the ovens of our hearts: what
counsel can be found in heat?

lovers are arsonists looking
for matches: beware asbestos
it's indifferent to combustion

# CRETE

Nighttime: we trade untruths
for bones. You lead me
through a garden of plaintive
ostentation. I look for stark
cardinals, but you show me otters
and possum. In the vinegar
of darkness, we are made vivid.

# ANDALUSIA

I.

partners in sunset
the owl and I in ballet

  he: the small flame in the wind

   I: the last tremor in space

like a tongue deep in my ears
the snow came from Andalusia

I survive myself

    I circle the summits
      of the depths I reach

        reflections of the hawk
     faint mountain silhouette

in what heart's alchemy
do I turn you golden?

in what heaven are you
sanctuary?

II.

I am the billow of a sail
bright shadow
of the electrical storm

beside me
the swollen weather

      I am the same surface
      as the sea gone to fight

the fossils
abandon me
to the lonely trees

we try to be a geometry

III.

an invitation to kinship
an invitation to the sacristy
      its door of yellow dust

the barnacle announces the debacle:
      I am the overgrown garden
      the broken roof of the abandoned chapel

it is no longer dawn in Granada

IV.

so I will grow fat
and die

the hawk, my vizier
I, his song

partners in sunset
silent sensate beings

[[[[[[[                                                      ]]]]]]]

we circle each other


*I am my neighbor's journey*
*of a thousand miles*

the sun bakes me in a shell
the carts of Compostela
        carry me to caves
                embittered with moss

V.

the owl circles my surrender
the sun demands a chrysalis

the blossoms

        (lacking mercy)

                gesture ineptly


    to see me now
    is to see a curtain
        of the mind

              a canvas of the body


Andalusia, like a seraph, stands tiptoe on its wings


VI.


the blood of hounded days
decays, reduced to a paste
of travesty and verdigris


someone is a ballet surgeon
      someone is a hand dancer
           someone balances a bowl of sugar on her knees


                    the moon is a hawk
               with its beak
           in my eye

## VII.

scribe of fire
        Velasquez beside me


                    on the opposite side of the river
            in flight beside the wind
the owl charges the sun


        the activity is continuous


I am born
        in the instant        of amethyst


*        *        *        *        *        *        *        *


a Bedouin holds a petal
                        out to the owl


the hawk bristles


the sun is taken to its butterfly


                    suddenly the snow
                    comes from Andalusia

VIII.

I lie down in amethyst

    all my dreams show
              black silhouettes of ballerinas
                    in tungsten and shade

      hawks retracing their steps

               a land unremorseful
               a sea unprepossessing

there is no weather
to speak of

except
        for the owls

              singing
              singing
              singing
              singing

              above their wings

# Augustinian Prayer Sonnet

Studious, yes, but hardly smart
her breasts were larger than her heart
He kissed her tits and thought of art—
Memling, Cressida, Jean-Paul Sartre
of marriages which fall apart
when whores are put before Descartes
of guilt which stains but does not smart
of sad bullseyes that long for darts
and so he took her bra apart
and took her breasts into his heart
into his mouth, into his art
the taste less sweet than it was tart
an act more foolish than was smart
which Christ had warned him from the start

# Rattlesnake Pancakes

I don't usually take bets,
but I took this one. Gobbo
bet me a melamite ring I
wouldn't eat a rattlesnake
pancake. Normally, I am
cautious but I needed a
gift for Emily Beth and her
father, being a miner, she
had a thing for melamite.
The thing on my plate was
as dry as a dying scab
and it tasted as vile as it
looked, but I got one swallow
down and then twenty followed
in slow succession. I felt queasy
but Gobbo never guessed. When
five hours later I was still alive,
he handed over the ring. I ran
to Emily Beth's mom's place on
Arapahoe. I found her sitting
on a two-person glider on the
wrap-around porch. "Emily Beth,
I got a ring for you." *Oh, Blister,
how ever did you afford a ring
of melamite? That just heats
my heart.* "Maybe so, Emily Beth,
but are you tepid enough to wed?"
*A gift is not a liberty, Blister.*

*I'll not marry you until Father*
*Life has sucked the selfish*
*out your soul.* "Selfish? Selfish!
I ate snake poison for you!"
*Yeah, but you didn't die, did*
*you, so what's the good of that?*

# MOTHER AND SON

I flew in and spent
two weeks with the
sentient patients
while she slept nearby
on a mobile bed.

Awake, she resisted
all questions refused
to talk, shunned her
past, shuttered
her early life.

I needed to hear
answers, information
but my request
was tardy by more
than a decade.

A fat madwoman
in the next ward
befriended me
so I engaged her
in animated blather.

It was not the same.

# WE DON'T NEED NO EDUCATION

You were sitting with your vexed complexion,
your dour shoulders, your hoarse aloneness
in the front row of my English for Unwed Mothers
class, and I hadn't yet read your essay on "Miscarriages
of Injustice," nor had you read Montaigne's "That Men
Are Justly Punished for Being Obstinate in the Defense
of a Fort That Is Not in Reason To Be Defended," and it
wasn't yet Thursday 2004 when we would be sitting
on the curb in front of The Sikh Community Café
where you were telling me, "The body is a lost temple
of bliss and blister," and the smile on my face was palpably
inapt, and I blurted out, "There's an ill energy that emanates
from your precise heart that I find attractive," to which
you replied, editing me with a surgeon's cruel disinterest,
"You mean it's an attractive ill energy," and I said, "Yes,
that's what I mean," though that wasn't at all what I meant,
and the sun was pursuing the moon in an ineffable dance
of unlikelihood and redress, and you were wearing
your father's shoes though I remember thinking what
large feet you had, learning later that that was unfair
and untrue, learning later that your heart, like all hearts,
was fuzzy, not precise, that your candor was a sham,
that you were neither a mother nor unmarried, that my
interest in you was not interest at all but usury, that I was
a man not in full but in fullishness, a false Montaigne,
whose chin beard, though elegant, was the merest bravado.

# WHEN WE MARRY

*when we marry, the river*
*and the wind will kiss, the sun*
*and the sea will dance, the moon*
*and the trees will sing*

      when we marry, the cornice
      will embrace the nave, the transom
      will buff the lintel, the gable
      will embark on the eaves

*when we marry, the wind*
*and the trees will dance, the river*
*and the sea will sing, the sun*
*and the moon will kiss*

      when we marry, the clavier
      will excise the choir, the overture
      will traduce the etude, the galliard
      will eclipse the hymn

*when we marry, the wind*
*and the moon will sing, the sea*
*and the sun will kiss, the river*
*and the trees will dance*

      when we marry, the fallacies
      will recede, the firmament will
      rescind, the moldy folderol
      will relent

# Asbestos Candlestick

- Love: the wound which never heals.
- We say soul mate. We mean self mate.
- Are there any pleasures not intensified by infrequency?
- It takes so much effort to be unhappy—where do people get the strength?
- Marriage is a martini in which misery is the vodka and happiness the vermouth.
- You never fall out of love; you just forget.
- It's rare that we shoot ourselves in the foot. More often it's in the heart.
- There's a succor born every minute.
- Paradise is comparative.
- It's impossible to feel through a scab.
- We say the sun breaks through the clouds when all along it's the wind behind the scenes that is orchestrating the miracle.
- When people talk about solitude, they are just making a virtue out of loneliness.
- Loss redefines need.
- Fire caused by lightning is indistinguishable from fire lit by a match.
- The ostrich puts its head in the sand not to be invisible but so that it won't have to see what's going to happen to it.
- When applied to weather, the words 'failure' and 'success' have no meaning.
- A life lived by whim is a life of nauseating incoherence.
- The ravines are crowded with the corpses of luck.
- Humility, the virtue of the repressed, is just lying.
- The body is text: life is context.

- There is selfishness and there is selflessness: there is nothing in-between.

# THE SOBER BOAT

I am the Advil of my beloved
and she is my Aleve
and when we are tender
that's just codeine

a bouquet of bombs rains down
upon our cathedrals
but, look, they are pristine
as on the day our egos had them built

on a hopeless boat
in a sea of sameness
the belief that change will come
sustains us

# POE/POUND VILLANELLE

The sands of time are changed to golden grains
the coaches are perfumed wood
and only thine eyes remain

A thought arose within the human brain—
be eager to find new evils and new good
for the sands of time are changed to golden grains

Not all our power is gone, not all our fame
so I will get me to the wood
where only thine eyes remain

Halo of hell and with a pain
ruffle the skirts of prudes
for the sands of time are changed to golden grains

Bowed from wild pride into shame
let us therefore cease from pitying the dead
when only thine eyes remain

A thought arose within the human brain—
dance in transparent brocade
for the sands of time are changed to golden grains
and only thine eyes remain

---

A poem comprised of lines from poems by Ezra Pound and Edgar Allan Poe.

# THE BASEMENT OF DESIRE

sooner or later you realize
    that all the leftover wood you've been saving
all the scraps of PVC pipe in the utility closet
    all the plumbing nuggets you've squirreled away
all the used sandpaper
    loose roofing nails
        railroad spikes
            iron filings
                copper battery caps
                  coils of solder
                      cylinders of tin
                  carafes of glue
            single hinges
        tubs of bulbs
      nylon cord
   bladeless hacksaws
rusted caulk guns
    bent nails
      blunt screws
        broken hammers
          brittle gaskets
             sleeves of galvanized washers
              leftover shims
           insulation kits
         cans of mineral spirits
       screen door hardware
     drawers of squeeze nozzles
   noxious solvents

the whole haberdashery of                    plastic pieces
                                        sheathing connectors
                                            and containers
is just a metaphor
                    of shifting meaning

representing
    sequentially
        and recursively

            your childhood
        your body
    your marriage
and your mind

# A Shadow on the Summer Sun

Shadows are so admirable in film noir
less so on x-rays and mammograms
What is a shadow but a white cloud
in front of a yellow sun?  For most
people, that's all it is, but I have
come to see it as an ominous
dullness, a yellow smudge in
front of the whitest bright
disc. That is singing, not
ringing, in my ears
The sad song of
spilt milk. The
soft song of
the yellow
sea. The
muddy
song of
dawn

One waits for dawn: it never comes
You remember
You were with me on the hill

This contemplation of the past is contemptible
beneath cowardice
but the future is fearless, the present less so

The
muddy
song of
dawn. The
soft song of
the yellow sea
The sad song of
spilt milk. That is
singing, not ringing, in
my ears. For most people
that's all it is, but I have come to
see shadow as an ominous dullness
a yellow smudge in front of the whitest disc.
What is a shadow but a bright cloud in front of
a yellow sun? Shadows are so admirable in film noir
so much less so on x-rays, scans, and mammograms

# Walking Coma

The doctor said it was walking pneumonia
    but Cid knew better. When Marguerite died,
        *that* was trauma. Run over by a bus. "Jesus!

I'm suffering from trauma!  I can see and hear.
    I can feel and walk around. Even talk. I think
        maybe I'm in some kind of *walking* coma.

One where I can remember but not exactly
    remember, communicate but not really
        communicate, exist but not fully exist."

Then one day all the symptoms vanished.
    He stopped using, got his CDL, drove to Reno,
        met a dealer, married her, even agreed to raise her kid.

It's possible to forgive the past its trespasses,
    stop seeing the future as a threat, reimagine
        the present as a goal. Resurrection—it happens.

# THE MAN WHOSE WIFE LIVED IN HIS NECK

This is the story of the man whose wife lived in his neck. Every morning, he would turn to her and say, "Hello, sweetheart, how was your night?" and she would answer, *Brilliant! What else?* by which she meant she didn't sleep a wink but rather thought unceasingly through the long darkness and solved each of the problems he would face during his day. In that way, he was protected from harm, and affection toward her swelled in his heart. What a comfort to have his wife not even a muscle away from his attention. Their marriage thrived, but unlike other successful ventures in the world, this one was never in danger of collapse. There would be no shift in interest or intent. Symbiotic happiness was the key, for he continually manipulated and massaged her, touching her where she ached to be touched, kneading her where she needed to be kneaded. Then one day, she informed him that she wanted to move.

"Where?" he asked.

*To the other side,* she answered.

"It won't be the same over there," he cautioned, and it wasn't. From over there, he neither looked nor sounded the same. Something in him had altered and not for the better. She began, though the descent was gradual, to sleep lower and lower. She rested in his shoulder now where he was meatier and where it was harder for him to hear her breathing. Her protection thinned to a threadbare covering, more irritant than asset. He wanted to dig into her, but she was impossible to reach, so deep had she sunk into him. Would it only be a matter of time until she completely dissolved and joined the others in his blood? Who would he look to when, in pain, he twisted and itched? Suddenly, he felt something behind him. She had turned the corner and lodged just below the hair on the back of his head. That felt perfect. That felt just right. That just felt fine. "Hello, sweetheart," he said, "how was your night?" *My night? How was my night? Dazzling! Just Dazzling!*

# Part Two: Interest

# FIVE'LL GET YOU TEN

And ten'll get you zero. Today's
the big race, but every day's
the big race. The track's muddy
but be thankful you're in the running
at all. BANG!!! *And they're————off!*
You're in the lead. No, you're falling
behind. No, you're pulling ahead.
Hang on! You're hard against the rail.
Steady, steady on your feet. If you slip
and twist an ankle, we'll have to shoot you.

# Two Weeks in a Dristan Land

when I washed up
alone on the shore
of the blistered isle

I smelled the bleach of burst anemones
the sweet arousal of the Dungeness crabs
the seaweed of sour twigs and feces

I saw debutante goddesses
abashing their swains
for what hadn't come to pass

I felt the uncanny glee of the solitary palm
the dilatory curiosity of the air
the aloofness of chimerical trees

I heard dolphins and swans,
aligned against integrity, conspire
to co-opt the sunshine and humble the thunder

I tasted hostility in the meanest weed
a cynical longevity in the beach fleas and swamp bees
a flash of happiness in the bold symmetry of the island flag

and resolved in my lately vacant heart
to replace Othello's handkerchief
to repent spurning Cleopatra the queen
and to restore the itching eyes of Gloucester

# Everything the Traffic Will Allow

1.

there's more to life than poontang
but not when you're sixteen and
your hands are full of heavy breasts

at the six o'clock when the sky
and sea turn green, memory
in a pencil skirt walks in

midnight daiquiris, the lingerie
dawn, fishing for kisses: the bugles
call and sound like hounds

2.

baguettes in your pockets, a broomstick
in your jeans, you think of films
with canine themes

the vile politics of charity, the bloody
wonder of the sun, the earworm
still crawling the corridors of your skull

if you're in bed, get out
if you're sitting, stand up
if you're standing, walk around

dogs on leashes patrol the lawn
an eight-year old rubs the belly
of a beached blowfish to make it swell

3.

stop staring at vacancy
accept the surrender value of your bonds
stop raising: go ahead and call

when get up from your stasis
investigate the trash: you may
find a rare Tonto thermos

think, and then think better
consolidate your outstanding warrants
adjudicate your selfishness

if you apply the paste of cohesion to the perforations
in your life, all that is written in the Golden Book
of Dust shall come to pass

4.

when's the competition?
rather, when's not the competition?
every dry peeled apple eventually turns brown

feel, and then feel better
buy something homemade
forsake the autumn mist

if you're sitting, stand up
if you're standing, walk around
if you're walking around, walk toward something

# No Hay Bandaid

Alone in the arms of amorpheus

I battle banal demons
who sit like grease
inside my blood

Pain is the saddle which rides me
Pain is the cowboy's grin
More morphing, please!

There's an unnecessary heaviness in heaven
There's an insufficient delinquency in hell

The Taoists teach that
a painted tree is as grievous
as false dawn

        but Buddha is a fireman
      and Vishnu cools the anxious
    plus there's Jesus: he cooks the books

As the stained-glass soul emerges from a covered bridge
it is chased by a yowling mutt
toward a nest of sleeping wasps

We have to mend the fences
whether they're broken or not

# EPITHALAMION

they talk but they don't *really* talk
she says

they fuck but they don't *really* fuck
he says

you've been together *forever*
the baby boomer says

*marriage?* marriage is passé
the millennial says

that that is *is*
wrote Shakespeare

whatever is is *right*
opined Pope

# BLACKISH BY REASON OF THE ICE

I was in the basement. I was in the basement
with Sara who was reading Job to the baby.
I was standing in the basement thinking about
Uncle Conrad's terrible black tie, 100% polyester,
which he wore to the funeral last Tuesday.
I was in the basement with Sara, whose
eyes were eyes of flesh, whose eyes were
like the eyelids of morning, who had made
a covenant with mine eyes, and I said to her,
"Sara, do you taketh it with your eyes?"
and she said, "What?" and I said  "Do you
taketh it with your eyes?" and she said,
"Stop being stupid, can you hold the baby?"
and I said, "I had not been as infants which
never saw light," and she said, sharpening
her eyes upon me, "Take the fucking baby."
And I took the baby, and I rocked the baby,
and the baby rocked me. And as I comforted
my son, and as my son comforted me,
I remembered they called Edward Dahlberg
the Job of American letters because he suffered
in his art. Many there are who labor like slaves
and suffer neglect. Does that make them Jobs?
"Sara," I called, "do you taketh it with your
eyes?" but she was lost, lost in the text,
and heard me not, and then, for just
a moment, I too felt lost, like a child,
like someone who meets with darkness

in the daytime and gropes in the midday
as in the night. Of course, I knew we cannot
order our speech by reason of darkness alone
any more than Uncle Conrad could've worn
a different tie to the wake, for life is wind
and death is astonishment. "Sara," I implored,
"take the baby for he hath made me weary."
And Sara took the baby with her eyes.

The title and many phrases in this poem come from The Book of Job.

# LIBBY, LOTTIE, AND CARLOTTA

Libby tried divination—no answer.
Lottie turned to numerology—a big zero.
Carlotta was interested in philately but she found that sticky.

Stay away from miracles, Libby.
Do not tattoo the future, Lottie.
What doesn't kill you will make you cocky, Carlotta.

Biology is destiny to this extent: our bodies
lead us places we otherwise wouldn't go.
Darkness is a long arc, my darlings.

No one escapes the entry into dirty sex
but you control the ugliness of the encounter.
Pain is never love—I don't care what others say.

It hurts my heart to read your poems.
You deserve a knight, a Christ commensurate
with your beauty, someone halfway decent.

Listen, there is a place where parents don't drink,
where uncles don't rape, where brothers don't die.
Where is it? All I know is it's not on the flood plain.

## JUST THE FACTS

skin cancer
walks along Zuma Beach
at noon

lung cancer
goes down to the City of Hope lobby
to smoke

bile duct cancer
bellies up
to Gill's buffet

bone cancer
rides through Runyon Canyon
on a gravity bike

at the hint of a cure
a thin crowd collects
on Figueroa Street

# The Autobiography of the Falsehoods Which Are Not Love

In 1990, his girlfriend told him she was seeing someone else. "That's OK," he said. "I just want you to be happy."

In 1991, a smiling woman touched him on the arm and said, "Don't believe everything everyone tells you, Stephen."

In 1992, he was generous with lies and did everyone he loved the favor of never telling anyone nothing but the truth.

In 1993, he wound up hating the woman he betrayed in his heart for betraying him in her body.

In 1994, though he tried to say what welled inside him, he articulated nothing and created a new vocabulary of pain with his eyes.

In 1995, he was palpably honest and lost all respect in the torrid eyes of the world.

In 1996, he got married and the past began to fade, like a song whose words he never really knew.

# ELEUTHERIA

Eleutheria, searching for asters
for the wedding of her son, bent
in the hedge and thought about
the letter she had just received
from her father. It was incoherent.
Was he failing? Could that be possible?

She watched an inky cloud suck
all the color from the trees. She
observed a conspiracy of garden moths
circle The Rock of Prayer. Walking over
to the frog pond, she stared at her
muddy self. Something had congealed.

With the wedding a week away, she saw
her childhood gone. And now suddenly his had
returned. Well, there was nothing to be done.
Nothing to be done and still so much to do.
She examined her reflection in the water.
It began to rain. Her reflection glared back.

# MAURICE UTRILLO

At him always, pestering him with unanswerable questions, why does he paint this, why doesn't he paint that, he doesn't know, he just paints, things that strike him, the things he sees, a dim shadow on a monument, twisted sunlight on an awning, the blue hieroglyphics of decay, a cat in the wine, the white endless façade of homes, the pink and grey of skies in love with loneliness. She watches as he stirs. Oblivious of everything, he rises, washes out his eyes, pours water through a spoon of sugar into his glass and begins to sip his pale-green drink. Absinthe makes the heart grow fonder. His canvas parts its lips and puckers. He grabs his Muse by the waist and pulls her toward him, presses his middle against her middle, his chest against her breasts, digs his fingers in her curls, pulls at the elastic of her blouse, her shoulders suddenly shockingly bare, her lower throat open to his open mouth, she's all a mess, dishabille, in disarray, his hurried fingers snatch the brush, a daub of color, a splash of paint, sips of silver, hatch of black, a wipe of white, lush squares of pastel tints, the second-story windows begin to form, enfeebled trees sprout up, the horizon is firmly planted behind the alley, around the corner, just beneath the burgeoning sky. What does this mean? *What does what mean?* Where are the people? *They have not yet been born.* Overhead, mawkish gulls begin to weep daylight into the marsh. The gutters blush as men in bloody aprons take their business to their walls. Priests in red robes bend their tonsures toward eternity, or so it seems to him, supine, head wedged against the bookcase, mouth agape, dreaming of dangers, feet splayed artlessly, legs perpendicular to the floor.

# ABSENCE

I am desperate in these seconds without you
I am frightened of miles and time
I withdraw into the dark imagination
where things are defrauded of their meanings
by a world of total frivolity
You anchor the real
You make love to the true
I am bound to you in consecration
You alone have given me weight
Without you I would rise and disappear
into the vast insensate sky

# STICKY, INDIFFERENT

I.

- Firmness looks like strength, but it's not strength. Contemplation looks like intelligence, but it's not intelligence. Kindness looks like love, but it's not love.
- We fall in love with other people when we see in them some version of ourselves. We marry the person we think we look like or want to look like. Disappointment in love is most often the discovery that our romantic partner is less ourselves than we originally thought.
- Time, like a dog, buries the authentic self. For the longest time, we're hidden beings. Eventually, our original selves, like splinters deep beneath the skin, rise to the surface where, if we're lucky, love's tweezers pluck us out.
- Caretaking is not to be confused with loving. Caretaking is what we do for those who cannot or can no longer take care of themselves, infants or the elderly. A lover is not a parent. A lover is not a nurse.
- If you get married because you want someone to take care of you in your old age, you haven't married out of love but out of selfishness. Misery awaits you.

II.

- Exchange of monologue is not conversation but queue of ego.
- Talking: exchange of solipsism.
- Real conversation is a dance in which the partners do not move gracefully across the floor of silence but step continually on one another's toes.
- Our love of objects is not the same love as our love for another person. We need two distinct verbs to make clear the difference. A man who loves his wife as he loves his car or his job or his lawn does not love his wife.
- The difference between mentoring and coaching is the difference between forming and performing, the difference between a kiss and a whip.
- If you want to know how tornadoes are formed, study marriage.

III.

- There's no real difference between righteous anger and irrational anger.
- There aren't kinds of passion; there's just passion.
- The Renaissance believed passion was a horse on which our intellect rode. We rein in our passions, they believed, lest they gallop away with us and throw us from the saddle, dashing us in the fall.

- Perhaps our passions are not so much horses as waves—rising and falling within us. We can jump them, or we can dive under and let them wash harmlessly over us. But if we're not looking, they can knock us down. If they're large enough, if they're tidal passions or tsunami emotions, if they're relentless enough and batter us in quick barrage, they may overwhelm us, and then we drown.
- A man falls headfirst from a horse, injures his spinal column and is paralyzed. A man falls off his passions onto his intellect and for the rest of his life is an emotional cripple. The first is Christopher Reeve. The second is Goethe.
- When you're at the end of your rope, get another rope.
- Sooner or later, the caulk pulls away from the brick.
- People who hate themselves have always hated themselves. Our capacity for unhappiness is established early on.
- Happiness sleeps with imagination.
- The plural of happiness is marriage.

IV.

- Intimacy is a house of toothpicks. It builds on an invisible center. It cannot be created by slabs of information.
- A calloused spouse: a soul impervious to emotional caress.

- The little bricks of happiness are part of the cumulative house.
- Intention is an applecart, continually upset.
- What is marriage? Seeing the other person honestly and continuously; never losing sight of the person we fell in love with; not being fooled by the disguises of mood, body, and spirit; not being hoodwinked by the vicissitudes of fortune, time, and circumstance; to see through the flesh of change into the bone of being.
- Marriage: no deposit, no return.
- Cultivate your spouse's garden.

# METRO RETROFITTING

Fax me back to the locked storeroom
where I'm kissing the hickeys on your back
while across the hall albino Flora sleeps in a narcotic haze

Fax me back to South Street listening to the dumpster
trumpeter, standing like licorice in the rain,
as the fetid officers assemble for the raid

Fax me back to running in the florid dark
stumbling like redundancy over stumps
in a stampede of buoyancy toward The Hotel Elsinore

# THE BEAUTIFUL MERCEDES

No one who saw the beautiful Mercedes
in the summer of 1966 could ever forget her.
When she walked into the Café Danglars, heads turned.

I was sent upstate for two years for passing unpopular
checks but when I got out I went back to the café
just to catch a glimpse of her again. It took a month
but she did return. I was there that day sitting at
the counter in my Bermuda shorts sucking a 7-Up.

The screen door slowly opened. I was expecting the second
coming of perfection. Not quite. She was bloated like a
bagel. Her thighs looked like freezer bags filled with dimes.
There was no necklace that could fit around that neck.

Two years earlier she was real money, a class investment.
When she ate up all her principal, well, we lost interest.

# The Ogontz Branch

There are stories I will not tell, stories I shudder
to remember. You'll forgive me for withholding them from you.
You may, of course, not tell me everything about yourself either.

A violation of intimacy? To me it seems its guarantee.
What I mean is we can tell each other anything,
but we don't have to. A string is stronger for its knots.

It's not that I prefer living in a house with a locked door.
That's not what I mean. What I mean is
did I ever tell you about the Ogontz Branch?

I mean the Ogontz Branch of the Philadelphia Library.
It was on Ogontz Avenue between Old York Road
and Limekiln Pike. Thirty years ago, it was old and run down.

It wasn't close to where I lived, but I used to love
to go there afternoons after school. I'd drive over,
hang out, read the paperbacks. No one there knew me.

I made friends with the librarian, a young woman
from Conshohocken with an odd, cocky smile.
Part of her job was shooing out the boozy bums.

It was in the Ogontz Branch where I discovered *Intimacy*
by Jean-Paul Sartre. A book of five longish tales,
the only stories Sartre ever wrote. With eyes blazing,

I devoured them. I ate without tasting, speeding through them
like a starving man before a meat buffet, but back then
I read many books I said I loved but didn't understand.

Back then that was perhaps the point—to race through the
pages,
to engulf, to possess the book—that, I felt, was the true thing!
It would be decades before I understood what I had missed.

If I am a book, I am *Intimacy*. Read me. Wrinkle my pages.
I am not asking for understanding. If you want to check
me out, ask the head librarian of the Ogontz Branch.

# Anniversary Waltz

She prayed that he would live forever
He worshipped her exuberant lips

She donned the armor of his arms
He rode the highway of her thighs

She climbed the hill of his condition
He biked the path of her delight

She broke his dreams against her fears
He cut his eyeteeth on her tongue

She planted the vine of his desire
He watered the garden of her heart

# CHATTANOOGA AFTERNOON

Let's talk about inconsequence, the muddiness
of sunsets, how the bench got broken, all those
things cruelly torqued by ambition. All right, all
right, you've closed the door, but you still have
the key. Did the decades have no weight? Is
time so subject to evaporation? Did I mention
that I may have to replace the dripcap
on the garage? Did I tell you I'm visiting
Lenny in Waterloo? Donna is pregnant again.
I still believe in regional happiness, you
know. I still believe in rebates. The kids,
scattered in their careers, are doing well.
I want you to know there's still a place
for you at the table. It's a new table, shiny.

# 1st and Goal

My grandfather was ninety three. My mother was sixty three. I was thirty three. My daughter had just turned three. Our ages were all lined up like the beauty marks on Snow White in the Donald Barthelme version of the story. It was the year the Bears were about to win the Super Bowl, the year my lung collapsed, the year my mother had lived one year longer than had my dad. I flew eight-hundred miles from Chicago to Philly to cheer up my grandfather. He was in a hospital with pneumonia. When he saw me, he brightened and revived. As a result of a mining accident in Odessa, my grandfather had only half a thumb on his right hand. My mom was also happy I had come in. As a young girl, she joined the touring company of the Philadelphia Academy Players but left the acting life after six months to marry my dad. My father, a shipbuilder, died from asbestos poisoning at the age of sixty two. I stayed until my grandfather was out of danger. Then I flew back. My wife needed help with the kids. My daughter weighed less than one pound when she was born. We never made it to the hospital. She was born in the backseat of our car. When I got home, I bent down to kiss my five-year-old son and my lung collapsed. They put me in the hospital and inserted a chest tube. While I was lying there watching the playoffs, my grandfather died. Two days later, my mother called. She had decided to fly to Chicago as soon after the funeral as she could so she could nurse me back to health. She stayed two weeks. When she came, she gave me a robe, glued herself to the TV, and got into my wife's beautiful hair. It was Super Bowl Sunday. My wife had made spicy chicken wings and zucchini bread. My mother was sprawled out on the couch like Snow White after a colonoscopy.

"How was the funeral?" I asked.
"It was just your sister and me."
"I'm sorry I wasn't there."
"He wouldn't have known."
"Still."

The Bears blew out the Patriots 46-10. Most Super Bowl sacks ever.

# Part Three: Accounts Payable

# The Vig of Love

Love's expensive. Who can afford it?
So you borrow from the bad guys, lay
your body down for collateral,
but the vig's ridiculous. No choice
but to pay and pay. Every day it's
just a matter of interest. You'll
never even scratch the principal.
But love's a gamble, right? Sometimes it
comes up red. Other times, it comes up
black. Go ahead. Put down all you're worth.
Hope for the really *really* big score.

# Rising to the Bait

1.

I am the minister of barnyard dreams
and it's my job to keep the daylight on.

Yesterday I was in Andorra
where I observed a young girl
perform her nuptials with a cat.

You were in a downward spiral.
I had to do <u>something</u> to get you out of it.

O, the protuberants of beauty!

*Idiot! Spit it out. What are you trying to tell me?*

Health is a cruel hoax.

2.

The crowd at his stoop refused to disperse.
*Open the door and let us in!* they demanded.
"A man's home is his castle," he asserted.

The Middle Ages had returned, with torches,
staffs, and battering rams. It was feudal to resist.
Other inane ideas traversed the turnpike of his thoughts.

To wit:

> Tonight I meet with Beaumont
> *sans* Fletcher. Sans Fletcher!

Attempting focus, he turned his eyes toward the long table
covered with platters of quivering snake heads; he felt disquiétus.
He was in need of medicine which had yet to be invented.

3.

I see that, despite my best efforts, life
will not be congealed. The future will
come to exist in bright, clear fragments
but the present will continue to be
a sylvan mystery, accessing a past which,
refusing to harden, can never cohere.

4.

*There's no gnosis like no gnosis*

A fisherman telephoned a fish but there was no one on the line.

# REFRAIN FROM EMBRACING

She had a smile like an ornate beer stain.
She weaved in and out of her intelligence
like a chipmunk in syrup. *"Pleasure,"* she
lisped, *"is too momentary to make me happy."*
She never tired of saying that or unbuttoning
the top buttons on her blouse whenever she felt old.
*"How can you not be attracted to me?"* she asked.
"Easy, I find you vile," I thought, smiling grimly,
pretending I hadn't heard what she had said.

Then she stood up and languidly stretched
and I felt a sunbeam fall across my soul.
My heart turned to warm water. I melted
like desire, like the Twin Towers on the day
after they were gone. I was optimism
hardened by confidence. I quoted Kierkegaard:
"Pleasure disappoints, possibility never."
*What kind of crack is that?* she snarled.

The Muse is a harsh mistress.

# O, Brave New World!

your right thumb rests in Odessa
  though your beard is on your father's face
    your wife's eyes lie in the clinic
      while your brother sleeps inside a quarry
        senility will enter through the missing tooth
          but commemoration will prove to be a brindled fear


      ripe dreams rip
        ripen into
      ripped dreams


          though Ashmedai has vaccinated the soul
          Tobit is still in charge


the hope of new emotions, you say ::: the kitten is in the mail, you say


        I say
        I know
        I know


    it goes without saying


      (nothing goes without saying
        except thought)
          thought goes without saying


    you were saying?

*the only sensible thing I did in my life*
*was to sire children*
*and that was my wife's idea*

1  2  3  4  5  6  7  8  9  10  11  12  13  14  15  16  17  18  19  20

you once told me
*every day the past is more*
*every day the present is less*

you told me it's ok to drive through the valley of electric crucifixion
you told me it's ok to live at the frosted edge of bewilderment
then you told me I need to purge hope's garland from my heart

# I'm Torn

I have to be honest with you—I'm torn.
Your waxiness is attractive. You have
just the right amount of plasticity to give
your sex direction, but you're a catastrophe.
I've never met anyone more of a mess than you.

You're monumentally, governmentally, inept.
You don't know how to dress, how to put on makeup,
how to wear your hair, how to stand up straight,
how to sit attractively, how to walk properly, how
to hold a conversation, how to keep a friend.

On the other hand, there is your nakedness—
I don't mean just your body—you are present,
available like no one else I know. You radiate
invitation and I find my heart saying, "I accept."

So I'm torn—I don't want to go out with you
but I don't want to go out without you. Inside,
I'm ripped. I can't eat. I can't sleep. Like hot bullets
my thoughts ricochet inside my head.

I'm torn—like a cheap paperback.
I'm torn—like the sleeve of a smelly beggar.
I'm torn—like the muscles of a sleek runner.
I'm torn—like a sail—like a banner—

—like a flag flown too long in high winds
  —like a bill taken out of circulation
    —like a yellowed map
      —like the tongue of a heretic.

I'm tattered—I'm sheared—I'm torn

**In desperation, not knowing which way to turn, the speaker seeks out the wisdom of King Solomon and asks what he should do.**

King Solomon: *Here. Take my sword. Kill yourself before it's too late.*

# CARLOS!
a palimpsest poem

The man and his wife were on vacation, exploring the desert.

    "Armadillos look like they would be lizards
    but they're not. They're mammals. Gila
    Monsters, on the other hand, are lizards.
    And so are iguanas which are domesticable.
    Nature has *much* to teach us. Would I want
    one as a pet? Well, that *depends*. It depends
    *upon* our status. It all depends on you.

    Tired? OK, I promise we'll head back soon.
    Hey, an iguana lizard! He's headed for a bush
    covered with *red* ants! The *wheel* is about
    to come off his bus! Look out, little fella!"

She looked at him with sawed-off pity.

    "Did you know that a castrated male pig
    is called a *barrow?* I had no idea. And that
    Barrow also is the name of a city thirteen
    hundred miles south of the North Pole?"

As she listened, her perfumed eyes *glazed* over.

    They stood, he *with* his hands
    behind his back, she with her
    hands across her chest, looking
    across the mesa, lately unlaced

with *rain*, prisoners of their own dry
dreams. "It was a mistake to have
brought you here," he muttered
to himself. "You're not interested
in any thing or any one. Just yourself."

Thirsty, she asked him for some *water.*

He handed her the blistered canteen.

Standing *beside* him, she was an elegant
cipher. What besides her looks had
interested him in her anyway? Perhaps
nothing beside his wealth had attracted
her. *The white* clouds began to thunder.
"More rain, I think," she said, realizing
that, though meaningful conversation
had evaporated more than a decade ago,
they would never leave each other.

Out of boredom, she started an inane
argument. Above the chocolate plain,
they squabbled abominably. Like *chickens.*

## GIVING UP THE GHOST
a palimpsest poem

Show me *the* sign.
Show me the sign of true love.

I'm afraid it's just an *apparition.*
I'm afraid it's insubstantial as a sigh.

Who *of* you know?
Who of you men know anything of love?

Look, *these* are actualities. Accept them
or reject them at your peril.

I am not one who *faces* facts.
In fact, I detest them!

What *in the* world will I do with you?
What in the world can I do with you?

For one, don't *crowd* me.
For two, show me you love me.

OK, here is a gift of African pearls
set amid *petals* of Indian gold.

An emblem, not a sign.
Oh, how you go *on!*

Love is not *a* walk in a *wet* park, you know.
It's not like it's subject to evidence.

You are absorptive and therefore your love is *black*.
I wish your charity was more active.

As the Jesus tree said to its disciple,
"Whatever is mine is yours. Take a *bough*."

# IT CAN'T BE, IT JUST CAN'T BE

The body has shifted into reverse.
The heart is inside out. The teeth
live in the gut. Both feet are in your
mouth. You cough out of your nose.
You sneeze out of your butt. Your
ankles have grown nipples. Your
elbows protrude from your cheeks.
You are growing hair on your spleen.
You have ears between your legs.
Nothing is where God or biology
ordained it to be. But still you get
served in restaurants. You're still
allowed to drive. People nod to you
kindly when you pass. This could
go            on            forever

# SPONTANEOUS TRANQUILITY

A shallowness: the surface stamp of who we are.
Immured to moonlight, the sea craves no human bones.
What had he held? A palpable ghost impervious to time.
The eternal become diurnal. The circadian become quotidian.

No roughness will she inhere, no fission inhabit;
she is deaf to dumb implacability. O, who has made
her sleep so deep? She is inevitably dispersed, existing
only as song, rising sharply out of magma and wave.

# CRANSHAW AT THE DINNER PARTY

Cranshaw leans back in his chair and cracks the back leg.
    He sits suddenly straight
        to hide what he did.
The hostess steers the conversation to the politics of bullying
    which everyone decides
        is the nature of the beast.
Dessert is served—toffee cheesecake
    with kiwi.
        It begins to hail.
"What does the future hold?" the hostess asks.
    Says Mark, the wiseguy:
        "Hands."
Morrie, the florist, offers:
    "Opportunity."
        "The reins," insists Bertram.
"The future holds the reins."
    "Just men?" the hostess queries.
        "No woman has anything to add?"
Cranshaw stares at the woman
    whose shawl refuses to cover
        her breasts.
He leans forward and touches her knee
    with his toe.
        "Back!" she yelps.
Bertram bellows:
    "The future holds back!
        Hahahahaha! Brilliant!"

# CRANSHAW ENGAGES IN DEBATE

They were discussing reincarnation,
what animals they would come back as.
"I'd be a vole," Cranshaw said. *Is a vole*
*even an animal?* Connie asked. "Of
course it's an animal! It's the only animal
whose name begins with a V." *What*
*about vulture? What about vulpine?*
"A vulture is a bird, not an animal.
And vulpine is an adjective, not a noun."
*Are you sure? Yesterday, I saw a hive*
*of vulpines in Oxnard.* "Adjacent
to the canines, no doubt!" Connie
went silent and stared at chain-link
fence surrounding the abandoned
construction site. Her iPhone buzzed.
*I don't care what you say. Canine* is
*a noun. I know it. So is feline. Vulpine*
*must be one too!* "Your sense of reality
is highly incidental." *Well, you don't*
*even know that birds are animals!*
"What animal would you come back as
then, Connie?" *A raccoon with razor*
*teeth and a keen appetite for voles!*

# CRANSHAW ON A BOAT

We are floating on the Chain of Lakes
eating Rice Krispies out of a bucket.
The sun is a soft lozenge medicating
a bright red sky. Water skiers hold
onto their slackening ropes like love
itself. On Party Island, the icy drunks
have seized control. Cranshaw has
his hand inside Margaret. No one
is shocked, he was born brazen, but
when he starts in on the Jews, Arnie
gets mad and pushes him over the side.
We let him tread water, then swing
around to pick him up. Justice?
Regret? No, Margaret wants him back.

# CRANSHAW ON THE ROAD

"Every tunnel's a piercing, every road's
a tattoo. The billboards are wrinkles,
road signs are scars. I saw eternity
last night wearing a sarong and smoking
a cigar." *Jaysus Chrysalis! Who does*
*this guy think he is?* Marty muttered
and glared at the broken line that stuttered
in front of him. Madeleine in the back seat
touched him on the neck. "Why so ornery?"
*Why? Why???* "Hey, lighten up. It's a long ride."
Marty snarled. *Snake belt! Zebra suspenders!*
*Alligator hat! His very being offends me.*
*The guy's a veritable catastrophe of badness.*
"What's that? Did you say something, asshole?"

# Whorehouse, Anyone?

*I can't believe you said that to him, Unc.*
*Really? In the limo? On the ride back*
*from the cemetery?* "Yeah, you know,
I thought he might be needy, having
just lost his wife 'n all, so I said, 'Dad,
I know this whorehouse on Vine Street.
You wanna stop by on the way home?
I'll tell the driver...' but he cut me off.
'No, son. That's OK. Let's just go home.'
So we went home, but at home I wrote
the address for him on a card and left
it for him on his dresser in case maybe
he felt like it later. Sweet babes there.
Sadie I had a fondness for in particular."

# THE BEST BANANA BREAD

Ed Raglan was a spoiled banana no one wanted to touch. Inexcusably br
the kid turned rotten, descending into dice and mash and reds and chew
I couldn't understand anything he said. Like "My car has acne."
He means rust, my father explained. Like "I want surgery
for dinner." He means takeout said my mom.
I flexed my ego. I dismissed him
as unlettered, a no account,
a rube. My arrogance was
raging and rancid.

The condescension of a thirteen-year-old punk has no peer.

Thank God we don't stay thirteen forever.
I thought my neighbor, drug addict, alcoholic,
tobacco addict, gambling addict, a total failure.
What of my own addictions? Who am I to judge his?
I thought my neighbor unsophisticated. No acquaintance
with literature or art, ignorant of any kind of culture or class.
Turns out he thought in metaphor, which Aristotle calls genius.
I thought that a banana that had turned black from age was garbage.
Turns out that sour milk and black bananas make the best banana bread.

# ADDICTIONS

- There is much more alcoholism in the world than there is alcohol.
- The women in the Women's Christian Temperance Union were all drunks. They were drunk on the idea of being in the W.C.T.U.
- Exercise: an intoxicant like any other.
- Immaturity: an addiction like any other.
- Those intoxicated by art or God never admit their addiction.
- One can be addicted to tofu as well as to opium.
- Obsession: a hobby on heroin.
- Pleasure is the addictive ingredient in all repeated behavior.
- As our pleasures stagnate or evolve, so do our addictions.
- Our pleasure thermostat is set in youth.
- Over time, pleasures congeal.
- The body builds in itself powerful pleasures—excretion, sneezing, rest.
- The hierarchy of pleasure is always idiosyncratic.
- Pleasure fuels the engine of life.
- Some pleasures are more pleasurable than others. If public service were more pleasurable than cocaine, people would be addicted to public service.
- All advertising is an appeal to pleasure and a warning about pain. Prostitutes, blackmailers, drug pushers, and extortionists mentor the advertisers and teach them the trade.

- Marketing: psychology for capitalists.

- Selling comfort is still selling.

- How hypocritical of capitalism to condemn monopoly and profiteering. Profiteering is the point of capitalism, monopoly its goal.

- In order to be masters, people so desire money that, to acquire it, they consent to being slaves.

- It's the twenty-first century and we still have maids and waiters and doormen and drivers and guards and caretakers and house painters and tutors and shoeblacks and prostitutes. Why? Because money is still the fuel and hegemony is still the car.

- Slavery can be legislated against but it can never be abolished. We're not just slaves to other people; we're slaves to our desires, our fears, our ideas, our histories, our genes, our bones, our breaths.

- There's no significant difference between the kid in fourth grade who was willing to lick a dirty floor for a quarter and an employee who is willing to do anything to keep his job.

- You can go through life with clean hands, but you do so at the price of the soul.

- Money may insulate you from dirt and the grime of life but not from the reality of the unsanitary body.

- The evil of money is that it encourages us to shirk our responsibilities, allows us to forsake our human duties.

- We pay others to do what we should do ourselves.

- If there's a collective unconscious, there may be collective addictions.
- Standing in a crowd: addiction by association.
- The mob intoxicates. The opiate is the people.

# FEALTY

tomorrow's work
I wander toward
a neon sine curve

I clutch my hollows
The future holds
my darkest hopes

a black gull dives
the cobblestones
my wants and needs

I should go home
the midnight dock
stabs my eyes

like a brick
my brother's pain
by fears inflate

a painter's gloves
deny the clouds
are not aligned

# CALL TO ARMS

As the commodities market is closed
for repair and as young girls in filigree
slips will one day clutter its brackish aisles
I call upon all cashiers in dungarees who bag
skeins of possibility to contact their flaccid
pastors who alert to maladroit nuance
will bedevil the stingy hinges to revision.

As the accommodation lobby is locked
for holiday and as fey valedictorians with filigree
degrees will one day flourish in its airtight
aisles I call upon the derided baristas in rags
who defend the multifarious flag children
to denounce the nefarious precinct captains
for they being overly gregarious will not serve.

As the consolation mall is marked for demolition
and as blue-collar bankers with filigree fears will one day
reconfigure its darkened aisles I call upon those whose
sinister principles tax the weakness of their conscience
to divest themselves of the rhetoric that bloats their colons
with Sagittarian wind and with unmatched debauchery
marry themselves to anyone spiritually innocent of crime.

As the turbidity district is targeted for annexation
and as the army of misanthropes with filigree
whips will one day co-opt its mosaic aisles
I call upon all those deracinated by dreaming big

and all those assassinated by dreaming small to burn
their fish-oil capsules to shred their certificates of privilege
and to reach inside alarm and pluck temerity out.

# SOMETHING HE WROTE

Mayakovsky wrote

> In the cathedral
> of my heart
> the choir
> is on fire

I just love those lines.
I just never realized
he was talking about

ARSON

# THE SURVIVAL OF THE BEES

I know the survival of the bees
is tied to the fate of humankind.
Still, a hive under the casement
window cannot stand, so, armed
with a can of toxic spray, I set out
at twilight to exterminate the nest.

I raised the can, but the bees
were gone. The nest was
empty. The pests had vanished.

Had they fled? Disappeared
out of fear? Had they, upon
some insect version of second
sight, retrenched with an eye
toward reclamation of their
honeyed fortress at a later date?

Or had they simply sensed
the crass inhospitality of my heart
and left in a huff of hubristic dust?

I brushed the nest from the sill.
It fell, a khaki-colored embryo,
onto the tough cement.

I raised my boot, made sure
I was unseen, and crushed
the layered honeycomb
beneath my studded heel.

Crushed it with impunity.

# THE CONCORD OF THIS DISCORD

-Love is a bottle
    unopened
-No, love is a skein
    unwound

-Love is a portrait
    unpainted
-No, love is a road
    newly paved

-Love is a rushing
    of blood
-No, love is talking
    in tongues

# Noir vs. Noir

You're sitting in a darkened theatre with Gothic ceilings
and one exit watching the latest Alan Ladd film with
William Bendix and Veronica Lake. Next to you eating
popcorn is a woman from Romania named Anna. She
is smiling but at all the wrong scenes. You put your arm
around her and smile yourself. Yesterday's plastic surgery
has been a complete success. The fingertip skin grafts feel
the best they ever have. Bendix, a narrative madness in his
eyes, is suffering from a war wound. He holds both sides
of his head and bellows, "Turn off that monkey music!"
The movie's good, but you don't like being in the dark.
You motion to Anna to go, a shade brutally perhaps, and
drag her down the aisle. In the lobby, empty but for the
concessionaire, she says wait, she has to relieve herself.
"Hurry it up," you mutter and pass the time staring at
your face in the mirrored walls. It's not your face and
that suits you just fine. "Where is she?" you wonder. At
that moment she returns. "What took you?" you rasp and
begin walking. "Hey, wait," she calls, running up to your
side. She's pressed up against you as you push open the
glass door and walk out. Something smells funny in the
night. It's your future, but no one will be able to convince
you of that.

# Part Four: Accounts Receivable

# Wanna Bet?

I was always more comfortable with the ponies than you were
more comfortable with betting windows and two-dollar bills.
A racetrack is a dirty, degenerate place.
But Dickens wrote about them.
And Degas and Manet painted them.
There is an electricity at the track that I love
that I sought out
that scared you.

What is the heart most like?
For you, two moons.
For me, the thunder of a thousand hooves.

During high school, I spent every Sunday at Pimlico,
gambled what I could
but mostly just hung out
waiting for someone to hit the trifecta
but no one ever did.

What is heartbreak most like?
For you, a baby skunk.
For me, a photo finish.

You came with me once
complained about the sun, the wind, the noise, the litter
the people who leered at you
the people who in a hurry to place a bet
brushed by you, jostled you, bumped smack into you.

How uncomfortable the bleachers were, you said.
How boring the wait between races, you moaned.

I like you, but we're not the same.
You're porcelain, I'm acetylene.
Alone in a room, we can get along.
Out in the world, all bets are off.

# POEM FOR DANNY

sometimes you're camping in Wisconsin
thinking about Melville and wondering
what he'd make of Nat King Cole

and sometimes you're on a job in Idaho
and you hear the pop of cooking soup
but there's nothing in the microwave

and sometimes you're in Lubbock
in a hotel filled with polished apples
and carts of recovered luggage

and sometimes you're in Boca Raton
in the company of salesmen
whose wives died of complications

and sometimes you're in Park City
harried as a lariat
lonely as a coati

and sometimes you're in Park Slope
staring from a convention window
at girders so innocent they seem almost botanic

and sometimes floating in the Gulf of Mexico
you close your eyes and let the water cover them
and then for a time which seems like mercy

you don't know where you are
or remember where you once were
or dream of where you may go

# THE ASSASSINATION OF SADAT

I was in the park with Benjamin
talking to the mother of a little girl
who had undergone open heart surgery
twice and now wanted to be a doctor
and there was a speckled dog the kids
were chasing into the baseball field
and there were screams and shouts
and the terrifying music of bullets
sung at a man falling under a chair.

I was west of the baby swings
in the park with Benjamin, standing
against the last of the green benches
drenched in the gray light of early summer
watching him for just one more minute
be a little boy, but what did I know?
Just beyond the corkscrew slide
the President of Egypt was bleeding to death.

I stood in the park inspecting the earth
where the children kneel when I heard a noise
and looked up. The little girl was bending over
the wounds in the uniform of the man on the stage
saying, "It's OK, it's OK, I'm a doctor."
The spaniel had his teeth deep in the arm
of the assassin who was screaming at Benjamin
to call off his dog. All the radios were tuned
to the same station. It was a chaos of compassion.

I left the world of familiar truths,
the world of boys and dogs and baseball
fields, a world where verities wave hello,
run after us, on our sleeves.
I left for the gray secret my son told me
that afternoon of open hearts.
"There are no parks anymore," he said.
"Only Egypt exists."

# THE HARDON COLLIDER

After I turned my back on heaven
After I turned my back on hell
After I turned my back on all worldly goods
my dead relatives all ganged up on me

    "Billy, Billy, what have we done to offend you?"
    *Go away, you're dead!* I commanded

Their neon green faces glowed sullenly
like blood as it leaks into the eye turning the vision brown

    "Have we not yet consummately earned your allegiance?"
    *Who taught you to talk so ineptly?* I asked

    "When did you lose your goodness?"
    *I liked you when you were alive. Dead, you're just inane*

    "We want you back!!!"

I realized this was temptation, completely naked
How odd its flavor—licorice—and its face—fearful
They all held out cats in front of their noses

    *When did hiding your face behind a cat become a thing?* I asked
    "What atrophied you? What atrophied you?" they began to shout

I had had enough. I knew what a bastard time was
and how miserable children can be if coached long, hard, and often enough

I felt like I was at a birthday party for someone who had not yet
been born

An indigent siren expressed its unhappiness

Somewhere a rope
was groping
    for its knot

# THE RISING TIDE

The new world is filled with old people
with good posture and a disdain for odd
postures. I'm just a rental dog myself
looking for the guardian of starlight
peeing on expired parking meters
and barking up all the wrong trees.

A decade ago, I was new myself. They
put me in the factory next to six-fingered
Marie and gave me tea biscuits and sugar
water at four-hour intervals. My hands
crumpled from the iron work and only
a jug-handle yoga pose could unbend me.

And so will it be with my soulless effigy
as proleptic ratiocination seeps into itself
and disappears, as the polished ego dips
directly into dullness, as Ivan Karamazov
deliquesces, as Imlac loses his footing, as Lear
begins to stink, as Pangloss rises again.

# LUNCH POEM

Reading the New Confessionals is like eating skirt steak
marinated in tobacco juice.

The tang's just wrong. And so the clouds vault
over the economy of molecules

and a maroon Jules Dassin materializes in the fog.
What price Edward Gorey?

Fax me back to 1929, the year of bluster, mortgage,
and William Wellman's *Beggars of Life*.

If only the lipstick sun would drift back
into this poem. If only...

but return, alas, is a hopeless trope
and the inarticulate cutters will never allow that.

Neither will the rash vases of the stainless moon
endure the bitter cinching of delay.

# CAMP ATHEISM

Forgive us our trespasses because they're boring.
Get off your high horse and then get off skunk.
Only vegan virgins understand how smoke gets in your heart.

Her verb was accepted, but his noun will be declined.
The determinants of fire are innocence and sentiment.
Executive summary: corporate torpor is now universal.

Clichéd as a butterfly as an emblem of becoming.
Clichéd as a blossom as a metaphor of maturation.
"A good poem is a mirror," he said reflectively.

Remove cap before putting on headware.
Do not operate while urinating.
And the bland plays on.

A tourniquet of roses.
We are not alone, not as alone as we think.
No one dies standing up.

# THE KNITTING NEEDLE

It was early in the morning when Lucien Carr stabbed
David Kammerer in the chest with a Boy Scout knife,
dropped the knife into a sewer, the body in the river,
and buried the dead man's glasses in the park.

It was later that afternoon when Lucien Carr
went to see *The Four Feathers* with Jack Kerouac,
walked to the Museum of Modern Art to look at the Legers
and turned himself in to the skeptical police.

It was a grey afternoon when Lucien Carr
holding a torn copy of *A Vision* by William Butler Yeats
pled guilty to first-degree manslaughter
and was sentenced to a reformatory in Elmira, New York.

The odor of William Blake hangs over this narrative.
Opposition is true friendship. Eternity in an hour.

# IN THE SEAGULL COLONY

They put my mother in a suicide bed
and rolled her in and out.

We'd spend a few minutes
together in the TV room.

I'd ask her about her childhood.
*What does it matter? Stop hocking me.*

A madwoman in the sentient ward
befriended me.

*Mister, could you change the channel?*
*Could you? Please?*

I tried to change the channel:
the channel wouldn't change.

I felt like a character in a Kafka story
written by the ghost of Anton Chekhov.

# BEETLE TALES

When I was a kid, nicknames
were all the rage. Down the shore
my friends were three brothers:
Mutter, Tato and Beetle. Mutter
was my age, Tato was in first grade
and Beetle (after Beetle Bailey)
was seven years my senior.

Beetle has this great idea: fill my pockets
with rocks and have me go over to the
Guess Your Weight guy. The guy would
guess wrong and we'd win the plush
skunk. Sure fire plan! As predicted
the guy guesses wrong, eyes me suspiciously
snarls, glares, but hands over the toy.
"You don't look like you weigh that much."
"Well, I do!" I shout. We grab the baby skunk
and scamper into the beachcomber night.

Beetle has me and Mutter lie down
on their second-story front porch
and shoot peas at the plate glass
window of the Acme Market. People
run from the store, pointing to
balconies up and down the block,
go back in the store, come running
out at the next volley. Hunkered down
under a nubby summer rug, we are
the invisible terrorists no one discovers.

Beetle wants me and Mutter to shill for him.
He runs one of the chance games on the
boardwalk. You throw four balls into a box.
The balls bounce and land in numbered
pens. His back to the customers, Beetle
pulls out the balls counting impossibly fast.
You win if the number is over nine or
under sixteen. Amazingly, it never is!
A guy in a felt hat takes a swing at him.

Beetle is pimpled, thin and very tall.
He wants to go out with Kay, our
sixteen-year-old babysitter. Kay
blushes but refuses. Beetle keeps
at her. Then, one day, she says yes.
The next morning we wonder why Kay
is crying and what those red marks are
all over her neck. "Chigger bites," she sobs.

Mutter grows eight inches in one year.
His parents fear he has cancer. Beetle
works the sub shop near the pier. He
treats Mutter like shit. One time Mutter
sat on a bench in the sun for three hours
waiting for his brother to get off work. I still
dream about Mutter's sunburned shins.

Beetle wears loafers with no socks.
He wears a half-buttoned silk shirt.
He brings a tall woman with teased
pink hair into our place, Pennyland
and gives her five dollars in dimes
to play Pokerino. He introduces the woman
to my mom. "She's an exotic dancer,
Esther. A stripper." My mom nods.

Beetle wants to buy the arcade.
My dad has cancer and needs to sell it
but sell what? Each summer, he just
rents the space. Well, there's the equipment—
at least we own that. For nineteen-hundred
bucks, Beetle takes twelve Skee-ball lanes
and a *What's Your Future?* card machine.

# One Sick, Two Sick, Red Sick, Blue Sick

I found a diseased fish
wedged between
some boulders
near the pier
I pulled it out
its left white eye
well beyond compassion
its shrunken shank
*nolo contendere*
I held it in my hands
as if it were a gift
from a maniac
I cut it in half
with a delicate knife
I lifted the skin
I peeled it back
I peered under
and all was…

sar**coma** sar**coma**
mela**noma**     mela**noma**
carci**noma**     carci**noma**
**sarco** *más*     **mela** *no más*
**carci** *no más*

sar**coma** sar**coma**
mela**noma**     mela**noma**
carci**noma**     carci**noma**
**sarco** *más*     **mela** *no más*
**carci** *no más*

sar**coma** sar**coma**

mela**noma**        mela**noma**

carci**noma**                carci**noma**

**sarco** *más*       **mela** *no más*

**carci** *no más*

I dropped it


It bubbled

stubbornly

among the rocks

# BEREFT OF DEATH

Had you survived, I would never have forgiven
you for not telling me how sick you really were
but you died so what's the point now of holding
a grudge? Let it gutter. Last week I visited a really swell
West Coast home built on a hill overlooking the Pacific.
I stood there and saw your reflection in the clouds
heard your voice in the industry of the lawn.

I met your little boy six months after your funeral.
He's a charmer, to be sure. So were you. May he outlive, even
outdo, his passionate dad. Maybe he'll be the future mayor
of La Jolla or be someone, like you, who rose in the world
on the strength of his sense and, like a telamon, upheld
the refuge of those who had no other place to go. Jesus!
I knew you when you were hale and stout like Cortez.

# Laundry List

- Water all the flowers in the graveyard
- Avoid the blisters in the casserole
- Of the serious and the serene, marry Mademoiselle Bagatelle
- Make sure to get enough sueño *de la razón*
- Keep a safe place at a safe distance
- Squeegee the walls of the shower of your mind
- Don't confuse the virtues of bananas with the virtues of banana bread
- Give God two weeks' notice
- Straighten up geographically
- Retool. Refrain. Repudiate. Retreat
- Do the left thing

# AFTER INSOUCIANCE

The clock had stopped; the crickets were deep in song
> *Save me from retaining mercy*

His face bristled with a hearty lack of affection for his youth
> *Save me from the nasty magic of the mind*

Charcoal as helplessness, the fallen leaves were searching
for another way out
> *Save me from stepping on other people's tongues*

If you see Death disrobe into a body, take the easiest redemption
the daylight has to offer
> *Save me from disabled attention*

Do not invite the caresses of memory into the house of bones
> *Save me from mere duration*

Do not believe the man who says, "I have the key to unlock Heaven"
> *Save me from the kiss of confidence*

There will come a day when the dust will not walk with its head down
> *Save me from the lure of lunacy*

When his skin was less virtuous, his ideas were a pavilion
> *Save me from early earnestness*

Cognizant of the mechanism of pain, he gave himself up
to impoverished need
> *Save me from late compulsion*

My body has a foreign policy
> *Save me from vile inheritance*

How insidiously failure inhabits the fierce insularity of triumph
> *Save me from accretion*

I have decided to drywall my imagination
> *Save me from desire*

Promise keeps threatening to cut its way into my heart
   *Save me from rude awakening*
What else is smashed between the flashlight and the trash?
   *Save me from my next best thought*

# BABBLE

We had a family copy of Isaac Babel's
stories out of which my dad would read
aloud when he was home, which, owing
to his employment issues, was very often.
I had no idea what I was listening to, but
that's just another way to fail to define
childhood, I guess. Anyway, the stories
were short, some just a page, and I let
my imagination sail away on some word
that jumped out at me (one always did)
and then, for those few minutes, I was
outside the battered gates of self, alone
in a city empty of rockets and God, where
I saw tower after tower of arrested escape.

# Trompe L'Oeil

Every morning he'd stand in the driveway and look out
beyond the maple at the empty street. One morning
he lost his balance and, being drunk, fell backwards
against a paving stone. As simple as that he was dead.
After her grief had subsided, the wife felt immediate relief.
Suddenly she was free to abandon or pursue loneliness
but that was easier said than done. For over thirty years
he had been a dutiful spouse. "It may take decades,"
said her therapist, "for the memories to dissipate."
"Make new ones fast," said her friends, "that's the best way."
But that too was easier said than done. It had been so long
she had forgotten how to remember new things. The past
had become a kind of poltergeist and refused to be dislodged.
What kind of life had she had which consisted only of neglect
and threats and the occasional fist? Upon awakening, that
was all she could remember. Nothing else possessed her mind.
His fingers still clutched at her from beyond the grave. That's
what she felt. *I'll never escape the horror of our time together.*
*The cell door's wide open but I can't even walk out,* she chided
herself. She contemplated suicide then reconsidered. *I'd be*
*worse off dead,* she concluded. That night, in a dream, she
was visited by the Lord. He touched her temple with a whip.
When she awoke, the holy world looked wholly different.

# THE KNIFE OF LOVE IS NEVER BLUNT

"Time cannot kill the cherished
tune, gay and absurd, and the
music unheard"
—Barbara Payton

this unmade bed, my life

through Athens and the Macedonian daylight
a cold night in a Cape May beach house
the twin pillars of your driveway

the pristine sink, the red fate
of anything ostensibly enjambed

speeding toward Center City
your shoulder by my shoulder
your hand upon my knee
your neck and my head buried in it like an axe

*noises. noises. they come to break the toys in my mind*

the spice! the bite!
the tang!
reckless
conscience
criminal
continence

*my mother was born in Trieste*
*got cancer which lodged in her breast*
*well, it grew and it grew*
*till it cut her in two*
*my mother was not from Trieste*


but we who choose to live in the center of selvage
and virtue

     and ransom

          and sham


are wedded to no such meditation
e.g., Melville's impatient agony

    e.g., Hawthorne's clear cold pain

        e.g., Millay's renascence of grousing and grief

# THE SECRET OF BELIEF

I don't believe in symbols
but there's a hole
in my living room window
in the shape of a bird

A hail stone punched out
the profile outline
of a nightingale or bluebird
or blackbird or thrush

Well, I have no idea really
I can't tell a robin
from a vulture
or a seagull from an eagle

A bird of some kind though
head, beak, torso, tail
with spindly bird feet
clearly in the broken pane

Were I a believing man
I'd almost accept
that there was meaning
in the shape of broken glass

But nature has no purpose
accidents are impervious
to intelligence

the random is no icon

Unless there really is a God
unless unbelief is a bagatelle
unless this is a true calling card
of the Paraclete

Listen up, archaic torsos—
here's the secret of belief:
*(but, sssshhhh, it's not for publication)*

**m i n d**

**y o u r**

**r e v i s e**

**m u s t**

**y o u**

# PASCAL

The large project, all over, over which he (Pascal) can preside no longer, for someone has moved the mirror, and assembling can go no further, had spread itself, like tea, a redolent chaos, on the floor before him, who calls once to his hero and is denied, which lay, like Pascal, like the puddle of hope, which man (or Pascal) is to take into his arms at the end of days, so he renounces food, renounces Pascal, lays waste the industry within him, within Pascal, and months pass, the night seemed the end of days, but neither he, nor Pascal, was any closer to the gathering of shards, than he, or Pascal, was to the gathering of smoke, and so, bored by relentless humility, Pascal, that transubstantiative miracle of the future, whom people ask after, to whom all questions come, Pascal, restless in his incapacity, incapable of the puzzle whose picture he can only despair, searching the reaches of his solitude, Pascal finds the strength to dissipate his confidence, so that notwithstanding a dim premonition of re-cognition, he resolves to try again, to understand the diorama of time, to step insistent back to life, beset by forces compelling him to triumph or fail, the parts or the whole, but his rose (Pascal's rose) is broken, and he can only watch as he walks to his brother's exculpation, to his own, on his own, as the map divides against itself making the decision in favor of lasting, to let the world persevere in jagged pieces, so time (as always is the case with time) lays him low, forcing him with exigent speed to repudiate his former selves, but, at being left to themselves, the fragments, one by one, rise in energy, reassume their fervor, leave him falsely buoyant, falsely pious, falsely joyous, in mute salute, in sallow soul, in flesh confession, which he (Pascal) feels in his heart began that night.

# NOTES

"Poe/Pound Villanelle":

A thought arose within the human brain
("To Marie Louise"), Edgar Allan Poe

Be eager to find new evils and new good
("Commission"), Ezra Pound

Bowed from its wild pride into shame
("Tamerlane"), Edgar Allan Poe

Dancing in transparent brocade
("Exile's Letter"), Ezra Pound

Halo of hell! and with a pain
("Tamerlane"), Edgar Allan Poe

I will get me to the wood
("After Ch'u Yuan"), Ezra Pound

Let us therefore cease from pitying the dead
("Homage to Quintus Septimius Florentis Christianus"),
Ezra Pound

Not all our power is gone, not all our fame
("The Coliseum"), Edgar Allan Poe

Only thine eyes remained
("To Helen"), Edgar Allan Poe

Ruffle the skirts of prudes
("Salvation the Second"), Ezra Pound

The coaches are perfumed wood
("Old Ideas of Choan by Rosoriu"), Ezra Pound

The sands of time are changed to golden grains
("Scenes from 'Politian'"), Edgar Allan Poe

"Blackish by Reason of the Ice":

"Blackish by reason of the ice" (Job 6:16)

"But now he hath made me weary" (Job 16:7)

"for we cannot order our speech by reason of darkness" (Job 37:19)

"Hast thou eyes of flesh?" (Job 10:4)

"He taketh it with his eyes" (Job 40:24)

"His eyes are like the eyelids of the morning" (Job 41:18)

"I made a covenant with mine eyes" (Job 31:1)

"Life is wind" (Job 7:7)

"Mine enemy sharpeneth his eyes upon me" (Job 16:9)

"Or as an hidden untimely birth I had not been as infants which never saw light" (Job 3:16)

"They meet with darkness in the daytime, and grope in the noonday as in the night" (Job 5:14).

"Noir vs Noir" conflates two stories—the story of the last hours of John Dillinger and the 1946 film *The Blue Dahlia*. Dillinger was shot to death on July 22, 1934 by FBI agents as he exited the Biograph Theater in Chicago where he and Polly Hamilton had been watching *Manhattan Melodrama*. In *The Blue Dahlia*, a famous film noir written by Raymond Chandler and directed by George Marshall, Buzz Wanchek (played by William Bendix) holds both sides of his head and bellows, "Turn off that monkey music!"

# ACKNOWLEDGMENTS

"1st and Goal" was published in *Atticus Review*

"A Shadow on the Summer Sun" was published in *Crack the Spine*

"Absence" was published in *Olentangy Review*

"Ajloun Castle" was published in *Eunoia Review*

"Andalusia" was published in *Up the Staircase* and nominated for a 2010 Best of the Net award

"Augustinian Prayer Sonnet" was published in PANK and appears in *Incompetent Translations and Inept Haiku*

"Auto Imperative" was published in *Scissors & Spackle*

"Babble" was published in *fwriction : review* and appears in *The Lice of Christ*

"Blackish by Reason of the Ice" was published in *erbacce* and reprinted in *MiPOesias*

"Call to Arms" was published in *Caravel Literary Arts Journal*

"Camp Atheism" was published in *Literary Orphans*

"Chattanooga Afternoon" was published in *Used Furniture Review* as "Let's Talk About Chattanooga"

"Cranshaw at the Dinner Party" was published in *Incompetent Translations and Inept Haiku* as "Cranshaw, the Cause of Wit in Others"

"Cranshaw Engages in Debate" was published in *After Hours*

"Cranshaw on a Boat" was published in *RHINO* and appears in *Incompetent Translations and Inept Haiku*

"Cranshaw on the Road" was published in *fwriction : review* as "Chapel Access", appears in *Incompetent Translations and Inept Haiku,* and was nominated for a 2012 Pushcart Prize and Best of the Net award

"Eleutheria" was published in *fwriction : review*

"Epithalamion" was published in *PANK* and appears in
  *Incompetent Translations and Inept Haiku*

"Everything the Traffic Will Allow" was published in
  *MiPOesias*

"Fealty" was published in *Caravel Literary Arts Journal*

"It Just Can't Be, It Just Can't Be" was published in *First
  Literary Review—East*

Just the Facts" was published in *Full of Crow*

"Laundry List" was published in *Festival Writer*

"Libby, Lottie, Carlotta" is forthcoming in *Fulcrum*

"Maurice Utrillo" was published in *Pirene's Fountain* and
  *Aeolian Harp, Volume One*

"Metro Retrofitting" was published in *Arsenic Lobster*

"Mother and Son" was published in *Full of Crow*

"No Hay Bandaid" was published in *MiPOesias*

"Noir vs. Noir" was published in *Aeolian Harp, Volume One*

"One Sick, Two Sick, Red Sick, Blue Sick" was published in
  *Exact Change Only* and appears in *Incompetent Translations
  and Inept Haiku*

"Poe/Pound Villanelle" was published in *Pirene's Fountain*

"Poem for Danny" was published in *Connotation Press* and
  appears in *The Lice of Christ*

"Rattlesnake Pancakes" was published in *Connotation Press*
  and appears in *Incompetent Translations and Inept Haiku*

"Walking Coma" was published in *Staxtes* as "Resurrection
  Happens"

"Spontaneous Tranquility" was published in *Pirene's Fountain*

"The Assassination of Sadat" was published in *Hayotzer*

"The Autobiography of the Falsehoods Which Are Not Love" was published in *Corium*

"The Basement of Desire" was published in *Olentangy Review* and appears in *Incompetent Translations and Inept Haiku*

"The Beautiful Mercedes" was published in *Staxtes*

"The Concord of This Discord" was published in *Blue Fifth Review*

"The Exit Towards Fire" was published in *OVS Magazine*

"The Knitting Needle" was published in *Blue Fifth Review* and appears in
*The Lice of Christ*

"The Man Whose Wife Lived in His Neck" was published in *Aeolian Harp, Volume One*

"The Ogontz Branch" was published in *Words in Place*

"The Rising Tide" was published in *Caravel Literary Arts Journal*

"The Secret of Belief" was published in *Olentangy Review*

"The Sober Boat" was published in *new aesthetic*

"Tierra del Fuego" was published in *Chicago Literati*

"Trompe L'oeil" is forthcoming in *Fulcrum*

"Two Weeks in a Dristan Land" was published in *E·Ratio*

"Wanna Bet?" was published in *Corium*

"We Don't Need No Education" was published in *Blue Fifth Review* and *Aeolian Harp, Volume One,* and was nominated for a 2013 Pushcart Prize and Best of the Net Award

"When We Marry" was published in *Pirene's Fountain*

Thank you to the editors and publishers of the journals in which these poems, sometimes in a slightly altered form, appeared.

Thank you to the members of the Poets Club of Chicago who workshopped a number of these poems.

Thank you, Ralph Hamilton, who guest edited volume one of *Aeolian Harp* and selected, tweaked, and improved a number of these poems for inclusion in that anthology.

Thank you, Joani Reese, Bud Smith, and Kaori Kitao, for your highly-refined and unerring artistic acumen.

The warmest of thanks to Ami Kaye for her faith in and support of this collection, Steve Asmussen for the cover, design, and layout of this book, and all the staff at Glass Lyre Press for their talent, kindness, and industry.

# ABOUT THE AUTHOR

**Bill Yarrow,** Professor of English at Joliet Junior College and seven-time Pushcart Prize nominee, is the author of two full-length collections of poetry (*Blasphemer* and *Pointed Sentences*) four chapbooks (*Wrench, Fourteen, Incompetent Translations and Inept Haiku,* and *The Lice of Christ*), and the poetry CD *Pointed Music.* His poems have appeared in many print and online magazines including *Pirene's Fountain, Poetry International, RHINO, FRiGG, Altered Scale, Gargoyle, THRUSH Poetry Journal,* and *PANK.* His work is featured in the anthologies *Beginnings: How 14 Poets Got Their Start, This is Poetry: Volume II: The Midwest Poets, Ars Moriendi,* and *Aeolian Harp, Volume One.* He is the review and non-fiction editor at the online journal *Blue Fifth Review.*

# Glass Lyre Press

## exceptional works to replenish the spirit

Glass Lyre Press is an independent literary publisher interested in technically accomplished, stylistically distinct, and original work. Glass Lyre seeks diverse writers that possess a dynamic aesthetic and an ability to emotionally and intellectually engage a wide audience of readers.

Glass Lyre's vision is to connect the world through language and art. We hope to expand the scope of poetry and short fiction for the general reader through exceptionally well-written books, which evoke emotion, provide insight, and resonate with the human spirit.

Poetry Collections
Poetry Chapbooks
Select Short & Flash Fiction
Anthologies

www.GlassLyrePress.com